# THE CIRCLING ROUND

## SEASONS OF THE SOUL

Poems by Joanna Nealon

The Circling Round
By Joanna Nealon

Copyright © 2015 Joanna Nealon
All rights reserved.
The Circling Round
First edition
ISBN: 978-0-9819797-9-3
IN Publications
14 Lorraine Circle, Waban, MA 02468

Cover art:
"Michael Triumphant" by DoloresRose Dauenhauer

# Poet's Preface

This poetry of "The Circling Round" is inseparable from my long quest for a deeper understanding of the spiritual origins of religion. Many years ago I embarked on the study of Anthroposophy or Spiritual Science, the work of the modern initiate, Rudolf Steiner, 1861 to 1925. An initiate is one who possesses the requisite moral strength and higher cognitive faculties to objectively investigate the super-sensible foundations of the physical universe. Anthroposophy brings to light the profound hidden wisdom which flows under the world's great religions culminating in the momentous significance of the Deed of Christ for Humanity, Earth, and the Cosmos. This wisdom awakened me to the spiritual nature of the human being and the living connection of the soul with the rhythms of the Earth. Another precious gift in my life is experiencing in The Christian Community, The Movement For Religious Renewal, the celebration of the Seven Sacraments, whose more conscious and enlivened liturgy was given through Rudolf Steiner.

These poems were written over a span of many seasons of the soul, some of them in much earlier decades of my life. Their universal themes are interwoven with my biography, especially the pain of confronting self-knowledge and the enigma of evil.

Another theme is that since the age of nineteen, I have been moving through the seasons without sight, a loss intrinsic to my experience of other human beings, nature, and life in general. I have also included poems to my courageous younger brother, David Nealon, who died in middle-age after many years of intense suffering, leaving a wife and two children. Of course, the book contains poems to my beloved husband, Kenneth Ingham, who shares with me the liability of blindness and the asset of striving to 'see' past the surfaces of things. Finally, there is one poem, "To A Child Unconceived", which encompasses our three wonderful children, Eleanor France, Melissa Jane, and David Michael.

Joanna Nealon

Note: Of the seventy-five poems in this collection, thirty-four have appeared throughout my books: The Lie and I, Stone Soup, 1990; Poems of the Zodiac, Cosmic Trend, 1992; Said the Sage, New Spirit Press, 1993; The Fourth Kingdom, Cosmic Trend, 1998; Living It, Ibbetson Street, 2004; and The Lesser Guardian, IN Publications, 2013. The import of some of these previously published poems has been redeemed through the heart's revision.

# Table of Contents

**Continued**

# Table of Contents

**PROLOGUE**

**THE CIRCLING ROUND**

In autumn I swallow the sky,
Not in one great gulp
But small mouthfuls, mellow gold.
By November though,
I am quaffing cups of clouds,
Then tankards of twilight,
'Til I am filled to brimming
With winter and the wide night--
A whole firmament of memories,
The inside of sky,
That for a space
Belongs to me.
Sun is my bright Christmas companion,
Moon, my moody roommate,
And Stars, my wise reflective friends,
Who, in winter's listening quiet,
Speak with less reserve.
But by February,
I cough up thoughts,
Reviewing mysteries, but restlessly.
A stream of blue escapes my lips,
A thread of sky
Which begs to be re-spun.
I clutch at Stars, but one by one
They flick away.

*(Continued)*

Moon is moodier than ever,
Longing for Her throne,
And Sun, the solace of my night,
Begins His swift ascent
To grace again the heavens,
Robbing me of warmth
And the willingness to wait for spring.
The sky expelled,
And I, a hollow cask
With staves of winter bones.
But then, an inmost Light,
Who faithfully remains,
Revives in me
The Thought of Easter,
That ceaseless Dawn
Behind all skies,
All seasons of the heart.

## NOVEMBER
## Month of "the So-Called Dead"

The leaden sky too often weeps,
And leaves are dead and lie in heaps,
And friends are dead and lie in graves,
As memories rise up in waves
And flood our hearts with so much pain
That we recall the truth again.
The truth that what we hold so dear,
The things of sense we see and hear
And taste and touch and call our own,
How all these hang of flesh and bone,
How naked sad November trees
Far long outstand our buckling knees.
You loved ones who have left us here,
Whisper a word in our soul's ear.
Help us in autumn's dusk to gleam
Eternal truth from transient dream.

## NOVEMBER
### Approaching Advent

An Ur-gray day in November,
Day of slate rain and perpetual dusk,
When memory is melancholy
And hope, an intellectual husk.

Gone the living flame of color
That lit the mellow mid-October mood.
Gold dwindles to despondent twilight,
And the soul finds real reasons to brood.

How can the soul's anemic landscape
Be suffused anew with radiant Sun,
Color spanning the heart's horizon,
Rainbow shine of human hope begun?

## READING THE APOCALYPSE

I close the Book of the Sky,
And I am in my room again,
Preferring to remain
On the wrong side of the firmament.
No "strong Angel flying through mid-heaven,
Crying with a loud voice."
Only silence
And the dark smell of dragon.
I am afraid,
But even more afraid
To read again in the Book of Becoming,
Go the long journey through thunder and blood,
On this most severe and sacred Path
Towards
Love.

## WHEN ON ANY MORN
### Christmas

Tired of my personality,
I retired from me,
Only to fall into the deeper tiredness
Of all Eternity
And my lack therein.
From that depth of infinite fatigue,
I see what I have been;
Under the poetry and the rouge,
My Scrooge persona,
The surfeit of silver words
And the penny-ante of scanty love.
And worse,
When on any morn,
From any flung-wide window of unashamed joy,
Have I shouted,
"Boy! Go buy me a goose and all good things
And send them 'round to my beloved Cratchit,
And hurry, hurry, to bury all my hatchets,
And Merry, Merry,
O, Merry Christmas All!"

## NOEL

I have been my own religion,
And I weary of the cult.
I have lavished the best years of my life
Bringing to birth
A baffled, mistrustful babe,
Wailing in a winter stable;
A babe bereft, yet sly,
Ever awaiting the homage of the three kings,
While I leave the humble shepherds
On the cold hillside,
Tending the sheep
Which were commended to my care,
Should I grow to humanhood.
O, where is my bright twin,
The child of light,
The one who seeks
In winter's deepest night
The Christmas Rose
Which grows in granite?

## SEEING THE SUN AT MIDNIGHT
## The Twelve Holy Nights

Now the Day of the soul, with its windows of Light.
In the streaming of Sun, the waking from dream,
To the merging with sky, to the surging of grace,
The redeeming of Night.

Now the Heart of the Flame, and its flaming forever.
In the Naming of Man, the mystery of flame,
Of entwining of Earth with the shining of Sun,
Man's highest endeavor.

## SNOW AFTER CHRISTMAS
### To My Brother, David

Snow after Christmas,
Falling on your autumn grave.
Yes, seasons will pass
And people will forget
The reasons for your life,
Your sufferings,
And how you fought to be brave
All through your many bitter springs.

But for some of us
Bright snow will never cover
Tatters of autumn,
The wreckage of your hopes,
Those last cruel things;
How you wept when Angels came,
Clinging to life like a lover,
Until you slept in their warm white wings.

## VISITORS
### Epiphany

Last night the Three Kings came to me in a dream
And confirmed to me
My penury.
"We have gold and frankincense and myrrh," they said,
"But not for her.
Hers is an empty coffer
That long ago was filled,
Til once upon a Christmas Eve
She spilled its treasures
Into desert sand,
And who knows
Under which of the many dunes they lie,
High mountainous dunes,
Which cannot be moved
Until the face of the Earth is altered
Or some supreme shift in her heart
Uncurls her desperate fist,
To reveal
In the center of her palm,
Minute, shining,
The mustard seed."

## THE WAY OF PRAISE

The way of praise begins to heal my doubt.
A ray of splendor reaches my soul,
Thrilling presentiment, swift and tender,
Of the Spirit Sun, Who makes me whole.

Long I fretted over God's offenses,
His incalculable cosmic crimes.
I, His creature, was both judge and jury,
Hurling my verdict in angry rhymes.

But praise, in a twinkling, sunders the veil,
Revealing Love's ever-blazing throne,
Turning doubt to deathless adoration,
And the soul's deep yearning to atone.

## THOUGHTS ON A WINTER NIGHT

Treachery ceases
When you
Demand nothing,
Forgive everything,
And listen only to night wind,
Composing on delicate chimes
The distant music of small children
On summer mornings.

## SILENCE

May Silence be my intimate companion,
My solace, my lover late in life.
May I burrow into its velvet peace
And cease my din, my long wordy strife.

And may I refrain from explaining myself,
From justifying my position,
Letting deft Silence serenely defend me
Against imagined inquisition.

May Silence bless me with a sense of hearing,
Love's faculty, hitherto unknown,
That I learn the language of other souls
And hear Love's voice, even when alone.

## WINTER REFLECTION

If I could turn my heart around,
How all my world would change.
Instead of seeing only me,
I'd have a wider range
To look into the circling round
That is the life of Earth,
To peer beneath the winter's crust
Where cradles spring's rebirth.

If I could turn my heart around,
I'd gaze up to the skies
And let the joy of Stars flood in,
To sparkle in my eyes.
And then I'd spy the Moon's caprice
Which often rules my mood,
And set that orb beneath my feet
And vow to serve the Good.

If I could turn my heart around,
Then my own heart would be
A Sun that spread its warming rays
To all surrounding me.
With Stars for eyes and heart of Sun,
Would come the deepest sight,
To look into another's heart
And read that heart aright.

## WINTER WOOD

Thick white cloaks embrace the bones of trees.
White garments for grieving the dead
In far Asia and this New England wood.
But these trees are only sleeping.
They are dreaming of the Sun inside the Earth,
Keeper of summer's condensed memories,
The fiery hearts of seeds,
Who humbly wait
To bring forth spring's renewing grace.

## A COLD EXCHANGE

Under a winter sky,
I confer with Death.
"Death," I say
"I have known you for so long,
And yet we are still not friends."
"True," says Death.
"I never knew how to win friends,
But I do know
How to influence people."
"But not enough," say I
"To teach them how to live.
In point of fact, O Death,
You are only another moment
In the great flow of all transforming
Life."

## MARCH

Someone said April is cruelest,
But March is the villain to me,
Winter's old bones still protruding
And the world decked in last fall's debris.

As drab and chill as November,
But then we were patient, resigned.
December dark was descending,
And starlight invaded the mind.

The night of the world is too long,
Then March starts to hint about day.
It teases our eyelids with light,
But Easter is light-years away.

The beginning of hope is pain,
Like March, the pale herald of Sun.
A soft crocus poking through snow
Is the heart, where spring has begun.

## SPRING AGAIN

Where to from here, old Heart?
Spring has you singing again.
But spring's a flighty soul,
Having a fling when it can.

Remember last September
When, heart-hollow, you wrote verse.
You were the husk of spring,
And your autumn muse was terse.

Spring again and you're sporting,
Courting a dream or two,
Like winter hadn't happened
And the thrush's theme were new.

But it's an old motif,
Senses' seductive singing.
You listen because you are
Deaf to Easterbells ringing.

## SPRING

The urge to lose self,
To rise, diffuse,
Escape like a sigh
Towards far periphery.
I put to bed on a worn shelf
My winter muse,
And head for the sky
And silver reverie.

Mother-of-pearl Moon
Welcomes me home,
Her watersilk beams
Blurring my memory,
And mild indulgent Sun at noon
Sends me a poem,
Repaying in dreams
The winter's penury.

First of God's reprieves
From grief and cold,
Spring tints hint of sleep
And deeper greenery;
Until the sky, alive with leaves
And blinding gold,
Lets my spirit steep
In cosmic scenery.

## IT'S A HARD THING

It's a hard thing
Never to look.
Never to look into the dreaming lake nearby,
With the birch
Stretched white and quivering
Across the water,
And the green
Made greener
At the lake's fresh edge.
But harder still
Is never to look
Into those depths
Deeper than lakes,
Eyes.

## MILLENIUM SPRING
### The Age of the Consciousness Soul

We sit on spring's thin chilly edge
With solid winter at our back,
A foul fifth season in between
When love is listless, pale, and slack.

The canopy of sky is low,
Long shadow of the snow-bird's wing,
And soul, a cataracted eye
That blocks the silver shine of spring.

The lack is in us, not the world.
The circling round is sound and sure.
We hug this season of unease,
The sickness that resists the cure.

We only love the outer sun,
The dazzling orb that heats the blood
And carries us from winter's rim
On senses' sweet and swelling flood.

The power of The Spirit Sun
Is white noise to a dabbler's ear.
Though Easter be all Light, all Song,
We do not see, we do not hear.

## WITH MY POET'S PEN

With my poet's pen, I poisoned holy streams.
Gall was the ink I used.
I, Judas, jaded with disappointed dreams,
From Christ's table was excused

And hurried out into the satanic night
With words in my mouth to tell,
Not for silver, but for spite and a poem to write,
That delight poets know well.

Soon my swill of words was spewed on a white sheet,
Neat, symmetric, and unsmudged,
And I scorned the saying as do all elite,
"By thy words thou shalt be judged."

## LIKE PETER
### Passiontide

There in the garden of grief,
Like Peter I could not wake,
'Til Judas came like a thief,
The Lamb of God to take.

When the crowd came, bringing fear,
Like Peter I drew my sword
And cut off the servant's ear
And heard reproach from The Lord.

As He was taken to trial,
Like Peter I followed afar.
It was not yet a denial,
But He was a distant star.

While I lurked in the outer court,
Like Peter I warmed my hands,
Craving comfort and support
As I loitered in cold lands.

When they asked me for my name,
Like Peter I would not say.
Three times I denied their claim
And was safe for one more day.

As they led Him from that place,
Like Peter I tried to hide,
But He turned and looked in my face,
Inviting me to His side.

When I saw He loved me still,
Like Peter my dark heart wept.
Then He went to Golgotha Hill,
Where His Holy Word He kept.

## TO A DEIST*

The God I know has human hands
And hair that falls in soft dark strands
Around a face, a face I see
Among the crowds of Galilee.

The God I know has pale pierced hands
And hair that hangs in crimson strands
Around a face, a face I see
Against the sky on Calvary.

Christ came to Earth, Himself to show.
The God I love is the God I know.

*Written at age 19 to my English professor, who espoused Deism, the belief that a remote divine intelligence "kick-started" the universe and left it to develop on its own.

## ON EQUALITY*

A black man's Angel is weeping,
Not just for the black man's tears
Or for the white man's sleeping,
Fitful with guilt and fears;

But weeps for the human spirit
That dwells on the rim of the Earth,
And none but the Angels hear it
As it sighs for its Second Birth.

A black man's Angel is crying
And a white man's Angel too,
And the Son of Man's great dying
Was for all, of every hue.

*Written at age 18

## EASTER THERAPY

A black stone lies in my winter breast,
Autumn's anger sown
And compressed to hate.
A seed is fire
And grows,
But a stone goes
Nowhere,
Could become a part of me.
I'd like to cough it up, shout,
Wretch up words,
All about the pain I ate
That never reached my belly,
But lodged against my heart,
A piece of petrified feeling,
By some black art
Diminutive replica
Of the stone that blocked Christ's tomb.
But my own stone looms large in me,
Seals up love in a small room,
Feeling smaller every day.
Can I dislodge the stone
By telling my story
Over and over
To "the piper I pay"?
Or is it only the Listening One
In risen glory,
Who rolls the past away?

## WHEN I WAS A CHILD*

When I was a child, I prayed to Thee.
Thou wast there, white, white,
Amid a wide and waving sea
Of lilies, white, white.

When I was a child, I prayed to Thee,
Thou was there, red, red,
And the drops that fell from Thy gibbet tree
Fell on me, red, red.

O let me pray as a child again,
Pray to Thee, white, white,
Pray to Thee, red, red.

*Written at age 19

## ANOTHER EASTER

Is it just 'another Easter'?
Time again to rise
A little way
Towards The One Who has risen
All that way?
So high.
The first to outfly Death,
That old usurper,
Who had never failed
Since he toppled his brother, Sleep.

Another Easter,
And just awake enough to weep
Under April rain
And the reign of war,
Just strong enough to stand
While the Gospel is read,
Then grateful again
To sink into my brooding chair,
Where I think my way
Past paradox.

## EASTER MORN

Thudding of chill rain
On the chapel roof,
Washes away The Blood Of The Lamb,
But not the memory of pain
Or the need for proof.

In this cosmic hour,
We desire sun,
The high festival of the senses,
Fullness of light, Pan's sweet power,
Not The Risen One.

Angels implore us
To commence Seeing
The Rescuer of Earth existence,
Who walks in the gloom before us,
A Sun-bright Being.

## TRANSUBSTANTIATION

On this unholiest Easter of my life,
I spurn the feast of Bread and Wine,
Spread on the banquet table of jubilating sky,
Food of the new Creation,
And attend instead
To the petty gluttony of pagan repasts,
The unhallowed meat,
And the heady wine,
That poison my sleep,
Rise to my brain like a lance of lead,
Slaying the Spirit Who would speak to me in dreams
At the sacred nexus place,
The chemical retort of Eternity,
Where Heaven and Earth meet and mingle,
Mysterious alchemy
Of divinity and digestion,
My angel and my anarchy!

## AGAINST ABSTRACTION

If I could perceive Angels,
Would I be standing here right now,
Landing this unwieldy poem
In the left field of language
And your indulgent laps?

No.
I would be kneeling in a field of white wings,
Learning to discern the light
And the mysteries of silence,
From which alone
Spring love
And deathless poetry.

## BLINDNESS IN SPRING

I went out in the April rain
Because my heart was winter dry.
Too long indoors with my old pain,
I needed proof there was a sky.

Rain seemed more real than sun just then,
Soft April rain against my face.
It soaked the ground with hope again
And made me feel I knew the place.

This was the Earth, the living Earth,
And spring was here to heal my heart,
And there was meaning in rebirth
And death had played its proper part.

I hated God, I hated Man,
All through that winter of dismay.
But in spring rain my joy began,
The joy of Sun on Easter day.

## APRIL

They say
That in the temperate zone
People intemperately kill themselves
In April
More than any other time.
"April is the cruelest month."
It's April now.

Can I embrace April,
Let its bleak beginnings
Become my budding grace,
Let April rain
Drench my dry black humor
In the bright waterfall
Of an authentic laugh?

They say
That the date of The Crucifixion
Was the infamous Friday of April 3rd.
Love died on Venus day
And rose again on the day of the Sun,
Self-destruct Eros
Redeemed in April dawn.
It's April now.

## FOR THE LOVE OF ALL

May I not love the Spirit for my own sake,
Clinging to salvation like a child to a rag doll,
Singing my brave hymns for a heavenly stake.
No. May I love the Spirit for the love of all.

For the love of all, may I outfly my soul,
Rising to the highest mountain peak past sky,
Fleeing myself for the Seeing of the whole,
Love's clear-eyed vantage point, vision that cannot lie.

And then for the love of all, may I descend,
Walking among souls, marveling at everyone I meet,
Finding at last the freedom to be a friend,
Bending to Love's first task, The Washing Of The Feet.

## SPRING LAMENT
### To My Brother

Dear Brother, I feel your pain,
Shiver in your winter never done,
Hear your tears in April rain,
Hug your chilled heart close, bereft of sun.

Not enough, a sister's care,
To bring back Easter to your face.
Christ alone can warm despair,
Can fire the heart in His Divine Embrace.

## ARIES (Fire, Ruled by Mars)
## To my brother, born April 3

Aries, the Ram, with flaming horns,
His questing head held high,
Strikes his stance on the hill of hope
Against the April sky.

His proud Ram's head is battle-scarred
For he is a fighter bold,
Butting his horns against the world
And refusing to grow old.

His love is fierce, but fiercer still
Is his explosive ire.
The Ram's wrath chills, but his love ensouls
The cosmic cold with Fire.

His will is strong, his heart is true.
The Ram does not take flight.
And when his head wisdom heeds,
His deeds are full of light.

## THE KARMA* OF BLINDNESS
## (Villanelle to Myself)

Because you are a lover of all ease,
A follower of leisure's languid way,
Wise Fate has kindly brought you to your knees.

You wrote the chart which cunningly decrees
The barring of bright avenues of play,
Because you are a lover of all ease.

You locked two doors and threw away the keys,
And so the stumbling step, the darkened day.
Wise fate has kindly brought you to your knees.

No friendly sight of faces, flowers, trees,
Adorns the canvas of amorphous gray,
Because you are a lover of all ease.

Yet gifts remain with deeper power to please,
The questing mind, the seeing heart, hold sway.
Wise Fate has kindly brought you to your knees.

And truth's pure flame, the beacon your soul sees,
Becomes a poem that banishes dismay.
Because you are a lover of all ease,
Wise Fate has kindly brought you to your knees.

*Anthroposophy restores to the west an in-depth understanding
of the Law of Karma and Reincarnation, the path of spiritual
transformation of Humanity, Earth, and the Cosmos.

## SAID THE SAGE

Learn to love your destiny,
Said the Sage.
Turn with gratitude
Each page of the proffered book,
The bright page,
The blotched page,
The many a smooth page,
The torn, the bloody page,
And at last,
The blank page.
Yes, thank your destiny for that,
Because the blank page
Is invisibly inscribed
With the indifferent, the outstanding, the outrageous,
All the pages of your book,
The book you wrote
And will continue to write
With ink from the bottomless inkwell
Of your sea of soul,
Your spirit depths.
So write then
In a firmer hand,
A cleaner hand,
And learn the lessons
You prescribe.

## WHO I AM

I am a stranger to sacrifice,
To honest self-denial.
Life exacts its own outrageous price,
A sufficient trial.
So I thought, through these slack middle years,
Until the flaccid soul
Knew its debt to life was in arrears
For lack of self-control.

I am a stranger to reverence,
To ancient wide-eyed wonder.
My self glories in its severance,
Ignoring psychic thunder.
So I felt, while selfhood waxed in me,
Eclipsing the Living Sun.
But my moon wanes without divinity,
And salvation has begun.

I am a stranger to compassion,
To creation's crushing need,
Too consumed by my pain, my passion,
To do Love's holy deed.
So I lived, through long decades of fear,
Fugitive from freedom's task.
But Love cries out, and I strive to hear
What the hurting voices ask.

## CHRISTOS
### Ascension

You are here, O Spirit of the Earth.
You live behind all seeming sight and sound,
And in Earth's wintery womb prepare the birth
Of flowering Spirit from the frozen ground.

You are here, bright Being of the world,
Yet shroud Your Sun in soul's ephemeral night,
Until Man's wakened will, its force unfurled,
Reveals to spirit's gaze The Christened Light.

## PENTECOST

I fell asleep,
Fell into an evil dream of the world,
The bat filled cave of the body,
Sinister deep,
Where Humankind and Creature have been hurled.

But now I wake,
Shaking off Eve's voluptuous nightmare.
Spirit Morning lifts up my lids.
All is at stake.
Wake I must, to trust and radiant prayer.

## HOLDING ON

Disaster, do your best!
You will not wrest us
From this soft chrysalis,
This transfiguring dark,
Until on luminous wings,
We rise from night
Into Perpetual Easter.

## REVELATION

Old dawns die on this resplendent morning.
The shimmering Air is alive with song.
Under the soft blue sky,
I am no longer a stranger
But am embraced by beauty
And the grace of new beginnings.
Today I know the meaning of the Earth,
The dwelling place of The Ascended One,
The very Ground,
His Body,
The moving Waters,
His Blood,
The Airy spheres,
His Breath,
And the inmost human Heart,
The shrine of His Dawning Spirit.

## WHO IS THE HOLY SPIRIT?

Who is the Holy Spirit,
We wonder this Whitsun Day?
We praise the Father, we love the Son,
But what know our hearts of this Hidden One?
Who is the Holy Spirit
For Whom the Christ made way?

A Wind, the Holy Spirit,
Who blows wheresoever He will.
And the way of the Wind no one knows,
From whence He comes or whither He goes;
But the All-Wise behind wind's sighs
Whispers when we are still.

A Dove, the Holy Spirit,
With His snow-white wings flung wide,
Soft wings, that waited to be unfurled
Until Christ's death renewed the world.
Then rose Love, the Phoenix-Dove,
Heart's wisdom to confide.

A fire, the Holy Spirit,
One Fire in myriad flames,
A golden Tongue above each glowing,
Transmuting base thought into Knowing;
No silver-cold tongue of old,
But the Tongue that speaks our Names.

## HEAVENLY BODIES

Stars are awake,
Lighting the dull crater of the brain.
Shine of our thoughts, the mirrored deeds of Spirits,
Weaving of worlds.

Sun is alive,
Warming the winter hollow of the heart.
Swell of our breath, encircling joy of Beings,
Abounding of life.

Earth is astir,
Kindling new purposes in the will.
Lift of our limbs, the fiery depths of God,
Presage of love.

## THE WEDDING RING
### To My Husband (June Wedding)

"The ring rounds off the corners of life",*
Two souls in a golden embrace,
That blunts the jagged edges of pain
Inside its consecrated space.

The bright rim is the heart's horizon,
A moving line that can extend
Far into love's limitless expanse,
Intimate boundary, without end.

*Line from the liturgy of the Sacrament of marriage,
as performed in the Christian Community,
The Movement for Religious Renewal.

## TO A CHILD UNCONCEIVED
### Eleanor France*, Melissa Jane, David Michael

You, child of my wakeful hour,
I hear your call from out of Heaven's womb
And am soil for the new life Flower
That springs from Spirit-seed beyond the tomb.

Descend by the Star-spun rope
And sink into the ego's earthbound night,
That in freedom, the hidden hope
Of your becoming bloom into the light.
Sweet Child, I shall tend you well
That out of dreaming senses you may grow
And rise up from the willed-world spell,
A shining being, ready to bestow.

*Our dear Eleanor France died on November 4, 2012

47

## CHARITY BEGINS AT HOME
### To My Husband (June Anniversary)

I will begin to love now, love in this evening hour,
Though all is ashes of roses, and I am very tired.
Words I will use like fingers, stroking a fragile flower,
Or no words, if I am inspired.

And I will start to see you, see you for the first time,
Standing in all your colors in the soft evening glow.
There harshness will be muted and beauty be sublime,
For your long brave years have made you so.

## SUMMER SOLSTICE
## St. John's Tide

We are all mad worshipers of the waxing Sun,
Devotees of light,
Bedizened by the splendor of cosmic day,
After sober night.

Once more senses' might crowns the spectacular Sun
King of creation,
As fey butterflies rise to His fiery throne
For immolation.

But something is withheld in our heavenward flight,
In spite of beauty.
We devout children of deep December-Earth,
Remember duty.

## JULY HIATUS
### Dangling Preposition

Between wings of warm sand,
A voluptuous vacancy.
Idea of a summer vacation...
Vacating heart
Or part of it;
Flung flat on some beach,
Seeing sky
But not seeing through
Because
You
Don't
Want
To.

# AUGUST

Soon your summer ease
Will slip into uneasy thoughts
Of early evening dusk
And work undone.
Duty will invade your drowse of days,
As the frenzied chorus of cicadas
Falters, slows, and fades.
Golden August will tumble to the earth
Your over-ripe desires,
And cooler nights will bring the nibbling knowledge
That you have spent this sultry interlude
On a honeymoon from truth,
The deeper reasons why you live.
But, oh, the pang
Of loosing summer from your arms,
Of rising from your bed of dreams.

## LATE

Late summer days,
Deep dusty green and browning gold.
That was ten years ago,
When you still wore August
With a soft elegance,
Wrapped its folds of sound around you.
Zealot cicadas
Lulled your cerebellum,
And ritual crickets
Soothed your conscious heart to sleep.
Now summer's wane has crueler ways
Of introducing winter.
A needling loss
Buzzes with the mad cicadas,
And in your ear, a static whistle
Overlays the cricket song.
The hum of time becomes the major theme
In Nature's dwindling symphony,
As walls of August,
Paper thin,
Let in late autumn's chilly sighs.

## VIRGO (Earth, Ruled by Mercury)
## To My Husband, born August 26

Restless and quicksilver ruled, but schooled by duty,
Is Virgo, celestial servant sent to Earth,
Preserver of holy order and high beauty,
His swift mercurial eye discerning worth.

Last bearer of the precious gifts of the past,
Yet preparer of the way that is unknown,
A voice crying in the wilderness, outcast,
Is Virgo, living in desertlands alone.

He wears Man's future countenance, the Virgin's Face,
Grave and beautiful visage, yet to be won,
Human feeling illumined by wisdom's grace,
The soul of the New Sophia, lit by Sun.

# CRICKETS

I love late August crickets,
Those monotonous musicians,
Scraping their sing-song fiddles
In proud upright positions.

When summer nights are sultry,
Ten thousand wee fiddlers will play,
Loud and fast and moonlight mad,
As though to keep winter away.

How sad their September song,
When chilly nights chase us indoors.
A few brave fellows play on,
Just a couple of slow encores.

## SEPTEMBER

Return to the chapel of the holy Dawn,
Where you find your way into morning light,
Your mind tracing the gentle lines
Of all the love you have ever known;
The faces of children
And the flowers in their hands,
And your face,
Lifted to listening Angels,
Who waited by your window,
Breathing joy
Because your belief was innocence.
Return,
Though innocence has fled,
And do not raise head from pillow
'Til you have sent your soul
To the kneeling-place of Day,
From where, arising,
You are free
To gather thistles
Or autumn roses.

## HARVEST

I fell asleep one night in June
And woke up in September.
The plumpness of the pumpkin Moon
Stirred me to remember

That fruits were full and round and ripe
And grain was high for reaping;
While I succumbed to Pan's sweet pipe,
The Earth was in Sun's keeping.

But now the harvest needed hands
Or summer's gifts would spoil.
The bread and wine of wilderlands
Are won by conscious toil.

Then I remembered friends of mine,
Who knew the autumn's worth,
Who worshiped at the common shrine
Of the Spirit of the Earth.

I ran to shake them from their trance,
But all of them had woken.
Earnestness was in their glance.
Summer's spell was broken!

## SEPTEMBER

As fruits of summer compress to seeds,
Condensed memories of Sun
Sinking into Earth's embrace,
So memories of my own being
Coalesce in clear cool light,
Falling out of dream-filled heights,
Into honest scrutiny,
September's gift of Self.

## AUTUMN AGAIN

Where to from here, old Heart.
No more illusions, please.
Autumn's an honest soul,
Scorning your summer ease.

How many autumns gone
And still no harvest in?
Just a lot of dream husks
And no seeds in the bin.

What will you sow this year
Out of your cast off youth?
Now that the dreams are weeds
Why not a seed of truth?

This autumn's sober truth,
The bloom is off the rose.
White winter's selfless deed
Is all that lives and grows.

## NIGHT SKY

A poet friend wrote of the night sky,
And my eyes thirsted for Stars,
Were blind as they had not been
For many resigned years;
So much had I craved the boon of Sun,
Dawn's rescue of color,
Shimmer of Noon,
Day's rippling garment,
Crowned by sunset's extravaganza.

But autumn and the mood of a poem
Reminded me of Night
And a young girl,
Grave eyes upturned,
Her gaze and posture
Hymns of unaffected praise.
She was ignorant of astronomy
And other limitations,
Lost in the limitless riddle of sky.

Like Novalis,
She laid her deepest prayer
At the feet of Night,
Sacred Goddess
And Guardian of the Light,
Her starry face,
Exquisite, pure,
Veil of the Infinite,
The Intimate,
Countenance of grace.

**STORM**
**September 11, 2001**

Loud hunting wind swallows the poet's voice.
Even politicians fear this storm.
The wind, is it our unbridled astrality?
Wind and war have conspired against us.
They have ripped the breath from our bodies.
Now they are hurling our souls into the storm's rage.
To have suffered so long this banishment from Stars,
Only to break within, before winning free.

## RETURNING

I fall out of summer,
Spiraling down, down,
Into fragility
And focus.
I stand at the portal of penance,
My corporeality,
And feel
Fear.
With the infinitesimal filings of meteoric Iron,
I staple my soul to my body.
Without Iron
I would shun my skeleton,
Detach.
But Iron,
Autumn's invisible forging,
Fastens my thoughts to world aims,
Wakens my heart to world hope,
Fires my deeds to world love.

## MICHAELMAS

I walk out under the October sky,
Free from illusion,
And hear dry ghosts of summer scuttle by;
And heart's confusion,

Swept from my soul on the clean autumn wind,
Blows with the leaves,
While memory that in time of green I sinned
Remains and grieves.

But grief is calm in this keen conscious air
And longing quelled;
That fool's dream which was all my being's care
At last dispelled.

And in my own lean selfhood, I must stand,
A leafless tree,
That each fall is unclothed at God's command,
Its sinews free.

All unadorned by the seductive spring
Is autumn's soul,
And I recall the great essential thing
Is self-control.

## LIBRA (Air, Ruled by Venus)
## This Poet's Sign, Born October 16

Libra is swinging on her Scales,
And she seesaws up and down.
The wind blows soft and then in gales,
And billows her hair and gown.

Oh, she is a rocking riddle!
Will she answer yes or no?
Or will she stay in the middle,
Not knowing which way to go?

But there in the windless center,
If Libra is standing still,
Indecision will torment her
And weaken her autumn will.

Poised at the top of the middle pole,
She scans the October sky,
Escrying a sign for her soul
Where sparks of meteors fly.

If she can behold the vision
Of Mich-a-el,* Libra's lord,
Then she will make a decision
And forge her will like a sword.

*Mich-a-el is the greatest of the seven great Archangels who consecutively preside over the evolving ages of the world. We are now under the guidance of Mich-a-el, the bearer of cosmic intelligence, in this crucial age of awakening to spiritual consciousness.

## THE DRAGON SPEAKS

Go, my Lizards, slither among mankind,
And with a wizard's tongue
Convince them that the universe is blind,
That they are cosmic dung,

Sprung like some excrescence out of matter.
Shatter the myths of old.
Scatter meaning into meaningless data.
Give them brass tacks, not gold.

Sound my cold galactic gospel loud and clear.
Pound fact out of theory.
And let the only mystic chatter that they hear
Be-- Timothy Leary*

Or some such other peddler of private dreams.
Psychic recreation,
A harmless sport, yet more useful than it seems,
For it hides-- Creation!

Hides from them that blasted lot of Angeloi,
Do-gooders, one and all,
Who want nothing but my empire to destroy
And so reverse Man's fall.

But when men are not content with cosmic dust,
Then LUST will save the day!
The id's perpetual pampering is a must.
Let brains and glands hold sway.

*(Continued)*

64

Rational self-interest, there's philosophy.
Logic wed to appetite.
Away with fractious Anthroposophy,
Which claims the heart has sight.

The heart, bah. 'Tis but a pump, a blind machine.
On this my plan depends,
The head, the tail, and nothing in between,
No center, only ENDS!

But mark you, Lizards, be it understood
That none of you impart
That detestable secret of Egohood,
Namely, the human heart.

*Timothy Leary, Champion of the use of LSD in the 1960's and 70's.

## MILLENIUM MICHAELMAS
### Age of the Consciousness Soul

Archangel Mich-a-el, You hail us from afar
On this world night of stupendous thunder.
We wake with a start, remember who you are,
And feel the heart's surge of hope and wonder.

Spirit's storm has begun. We must not sleep again
Or be dazed by dreams, as always before.
Earth sends forth a cry as the sky cracks open
And waves of spirit break on every shore.

Your mighty image forms, filling the night sky,
Spirit's clear beacon in the fearful dark.
Your blazing hand upraised, you urge our human I
To kindle from your fire Love's inmost spark.

## ON THE EVE OF WAR

Make no plans
But the plan of love.
Draw up blueprints for beginnings
That do not end with you.
There is no return to The Garden,
The place of the holy dream
Where two dwelt.
We are awake now,
And we are many.
The City has something for everyone
And room for all,
Except those
Who build tall towers in the desert,
Far from The City
And peace.

## REMEMBERING MICHAELMAS
### Late Autumn

Standing among tatters of trees,
Ankle-deep in cracking corpses of leaves,
One sees tatters of old resolves,
Last year's ideals deceased, and the soul grieves.

Feet that once found a clear pathway
Now only wander down disheveled streets,
Strewn with debris of destiny
And the bruised fallen fruit that no one eats.

But startled by nature's death mask
As harsh mirror of self-discovery,
The soul stirs, and shaken from trance,
Wakens the will to its recovery!

Then Spirit's blaze consumes dead leaves,
Selfish motives that litter the soul's ground,
And fiery seeds of will are sown,
Bright sparks of spring, so Easter may abound.

## THE MERRY PASSENGER*
## To My Husband

You are my ark,
My anchored ship,
The strong deck where I dance.
Between storms
I have this chance to love you,
Before the rising sea
Lifts your anchor like a toy,
And irresistible currents
Chart your course.
I want to stay on board,
Not just as merry passenger,
But worthy shipmate,
Womanning your decks,
Holding the wheel,
When seas run high;
Until at length,
We sail unseen
Between Scylla and Charybdis.

*My husband, the scientist and businessman,
and I, the indigent poet, the merry, at times 'un-merry',
passenger.

## AFTERWARD TO AGONY
### To My Brother

You were Fire,
Fire and Love,
Though Love's countenance could be distorted,
Fire dimmed,
By unremitting pain.
But set free,
You are flame again,
Clear shining,
An intense and tender ray,
Lighting the night corners of our hearts,
Warming us on our way.

## BLINDNESS IN AUTUMN

It doesn't hurt to be blind in the fall
As much as it does in spring,
Though autumn's the loveliest season of all
While the colors have their fling.

But as soon as Scorpio follows the Scales,
When the robe of Earth is a rag,
Then the eye of the soul drops the last of its veils,
And the world is a withered hag.

But the soul's clear sight is as keen as a knife,
And pierces the crust of the Earth,
And there in the grave of the world lies Life,
The sunbright seeds of rebirth.

O, winter brings death and blindness is drear,
But the soul is a lively being
And shines like a star in the dark of the year,
For night is the best time for Seeing.

## INITIATION*

Behind the veil, the human soul looks out
And finding sense-bedimmed the world without,
Then inward turns to wake the primal eye
That pierces Earth and enigmatic sky.
But eyes of Spirit like the eyes of Earth
Are wholly blind before their hour of birth,
And just as pain precedes new life unfolding,
So pain brings forth the Spirit's new beholding;
The pain of perfect honesty within
That tears away the soul's deceptive skin,
The pain of leaving all that's known and dear
To face worst pain of all, the pain of fear.
For we must swim through fear as through a sea
Before we gain the shore of certainty,
The certainty of Living Spirit's Might
Which weaves the world from looms of Love and Light,
Of Hosts in Earth and Water, Fire and Air,
Who keep all life though we be unaware,
Of Spirits Who from Sun and Moon bestow
The cosmic balance wherein we may grow,
Wrapped for a time within the senses' web
That memory of the sight of Spirit ebb,
To be regained through Christ in future hour,
Who graces us with free and conscious power.
The inner eye was not asleep in Man
When humming of Creation first began.
Our feeble outer eye could scarce perceive
The forms of sense to which we now so cleave.

*(Continued)*

We saw, as in a dream, the real events,
The deeds of God behind the world of sense.
We saw the Spirit-brightness of the Sun
Before eclipse of Godhead had begun.
O cruel eclipse that shrouds the soul in haze,
While sharpening the vulgar outer gaze.
We were made blind in order that we 'see'.
What answer to this cosmic riddle be?
The wakened soul now sees the sacred sight
Of Man's ascent from darkness into Light,
Our selfhood born within a world of death,
Our conscious being felt through blood and breath,
Our spirit flashing forth from out the dark
From God's own Fire, yet a separate spark.
For Freedom's sake Man suffers chains of Earth,
For only Freedom gives to Love its worth!

*Written at age 30, when I had the presumption to attempt a
summary of the great principle of initiation and the spiritual
evolution of human consciousness 'in couplets'!

## LEARNING TO TELL TIME

The time of Blood is over.
Blood told us
Who we were,
How to live.
But Blood is silent now.
Silent in the morning, the afternoon,
And even at night.
The begetting Moon no longer rules
But is seen as what it is,
A sacred promise
Of the Sun's golden clarity.
Stepping forth from the dream of Night,
The self stands juxta-posed
To the fierce in-gatherings of Group Souls.
The self is its own unique species
And bears allegiance to all.
Its mission is Love,
Lifted from instinctive depths
To freedom's conscious heights.

## THE TENTH HIERARCHY

From exalted Seraphim,
Spirits of Love,
Nearest to God,
To attentive Angels,
Spirits of Twilight,
Nearest to Man,
Nine great Hierarchies.
But what of the tenth?
Ten is the perfect number,
Sum of completion
And thus of new beginnings!
Who will be The Tenth Hierarchy?
"The whole Creation groans and travails...
Waiting for The Adoption."

## BEYOND ASTRONOMY

The heart is the lens
For the real sky,
Not the touted telescope
Or the intrusive satellite,
An affront to stars,
Or even the naked eye,
Mere spectator
Of manifest beauty.

Through the heart's clear glass,
Shines the gaze of the Hierarchies,
Spirits of Stars,
Weavers of Worlds,
Molders of Form,
Upholders of Life.
Long and deeply they look,
Waiting, waiting,
For the heart to see.

## COMMENCEMENT

At every moment,
I can begin the long ascent,
Can place my foot
On the humblest rung of high intent,
A quiet motion.
Like setting out to count the stars,
I begin with one.
Why stand idle then?
Why not bestir God-given powers
For that small step
Which commits to Consecration?
Man's toil of love,
The patient rescue of Creation,
Begun by Christ.

# EPILOGUE

## IN CHRISTO MORIMUR

Here we are, half dead with grief and age,
Yet more alive than we have ever been.
Our futile masks of pride have slipped,
And we begin to speak each other's Names.
Bearing with grace the exigent winter,
We do not "rage against the dying..."*
As the world contracts,
The heart expands,
As the body dims,
The spirit flames,
And We Will See The Sun At Midnight.

*Dylan Thomas's "Do not Go Gentle into That Good Night"

## About the Poet

I grew up, the third of five children, in an old houseboat on Ash Creek in Bridgeport, Connecticut. At age seventeen I learned I had a serious eye condition and two years later I woke up one morning without my sight. It was after this loss that I encountered so many inspiring people who would change my life completely, beginning with my husband, Kenneth Ingham, also newly blinded, who I met at The Carroll Center for the Blind in Newton, Massachusetts.

I received a B.A. in French Literature from the just budding University of Bridgeport on Long Island Sound, where classes were held in charming old mansions. With the help and encouragement of my remarkable French professor, Dr. John Rassias, I won a Fulbright Scholarship to study at the Sorbonne in Paris. Dr. Rassias went on to an extraordinary career at Dartmouth, where he is renowned for his dynamic language-teaching techniques and his work as head of the Peace Corps for the Francophone countries in Africa. My husband obtained a Ph.D. in Physics from Brandeis University and became an entrepreneur, while I 'went on' to the challenge and delight of bringing up three children and writing lots of poetry.

Including this collection, I have seven published books (see note after preface for titles) and three more awaiting publication. Over the years, I have had the honor of reciting at various wonderful venues in Massachusetts, such as Tapestry of Voices (Annual April Poetry Festival at the B.P.L), Stone Soup, Ibbetson Street, Walden Pond, Chapter and Verse, Main Street Cafés©, and Newton and Brocton Library Series. In addition, since 1992 I have participated in poetry programs at Norfolk and Bay State Prisons.

As indicated in my preface, my husband and I have followed the golden thread of Anthroposophy, the work of Rudolf Steiner, 1861 to 1925. Some fruits of Anthroposophy for the world are Waldorf Education, Bio-Dynamic Farming, Anthroposophical Medicine, Camphill Movement for special-needs children and adults, the Arts of Eurythmy, Speech Formation, Drama, painting, and architecture, as well as the afore mentioned Christian Community, The Movement For Religious Renewal.

I have asked my husband, who years ago kindly appointed himself my 'agent', to refrain from seeking reviews for THE CIRCLING ROUND. I offer this compendium of poems in a spirit of deep gratitude for all I have received from the wisdom of Anthroposophy and the resurrection forces of The Christian Community, as well as the treasured companionship of family and friends in destiny.

Joanna Nealon

www.ingramcontent.com/pod-product-compliance
Lightning Source LLC
Chambersburg PA
CBHW071624040426
42452CB00009B/1473